MW01598461

# NO GRAINER BAKER

Copyright © Ann Preston, 2012
First Edition, 2012
All rights reserved

Recipes created and written by: Ann Preston
Campbellford, Ontario, Canada

Photography by: Julie Fairservice
Hastings, Ontario, Canada

I.S.B.N. 13-978-1478268840

# Dedication

For my husband Doug, who has been my biggest supporter and fan of my baked goods over the years. His willingness to try anything and give his honest opinion helped get me this far.

And to both of my sons Matthew and Andrew who never said "no" to anything I made them.

A special thanks to my friend Julie Fairservice who without her help and determination I would not have completed this project.

# WHY I CREATED THIS BOOK

My health changed the winter of 2012, when my fitness instructor put out a challenge to give up wheat and if possible, all grains. She suggested reading 'Wheat Belly' by William Davis as a source of information. I had given up wheat a few years earlier and really didn't find it too difficult as I substituted spelt and quinoa flour for wheat with good results. Eliminating all grains was going to be more difficult as I believed this meant no more muffins and cookies at lunch and snacks, no more crackers with hummus and most of all no more sandwiches. Wow, this was not going to be easy. Then I read 'Wheat Belly' and decided to make this lifestyle choice. I have had a history of digestive problems and thought giving up all grains might help. My next challenge was convincing my husband of 35 years, that this would be beneficial for his health. He loved his breads and enjoyed them for breakfast, lunch and supper. He also loved cookies, cakes, muffins and pie - a true carboholic! His blood pressure and cholesterol were creeping up; he had been gaining weight and had less energy.

It was then that I created the 'No Bran Bran Muffins'. Not only were they much like the original, my husband said they were even better. I knew then if I could replace our other favourites with no grain baking, that we were on the road to success.

Flushed with success I decided to try other things like cakes and cookies. Not everything turned out the first, second, third and sometimes fourth attempt but I have never backed away from a baking challenge. At first I just wanted to create grain free recipes for my family, to improve their health. But when I started giving out samples, the feedback was so positive that I wanted to share them with others. It didn't take long until I decided to publish a recipe book for those interested in grain free recipes. Although the recipes are ideal for those with celiac disease, it is also beneficial for those wanting to decrease the carbohydrates or increase the fibre in their diets. I soon realized these recipes were targeting a now large group of people who are pre- diabetic, diabetic, celiac, or who have heart disease. And one of the biggest concerns many people have is finding foods and recipes that are tasty and delicious and allow them to stick to healthy eating for life.

My hope is that these recipes, which I have tried to make as simple as possible, help those who need to make changes and be able to serve them to family and friends without anyone knowing they are healthy. My husband would be the first to say, "This stuff is so good even a carboholic doesn't know they are eating healthy food!" That is the best testimonial I can give you. My husband and I have noticed continued health improvements, the longer we stick with this new lifestyle. One of the biggest changes for me is not being hungry all the time. I literally had to eat every 2 hours; now I can go from meal to meal without constantly snacking. I can honestly say, staying with this diet is a "NO BRAINER".

I hope you enjoy these recipes as much as my family and friends that have been my tasters during the period of creating the book. I encourage you to go beyond the muffins, cakes and cookie recipes and try the crackers, which everyone has said are amazing, and piecrust that my husband gave a two thumbs up. You'll be surprised at how easy these recipes are to make, so don't be intimidated by the title.

# HELPFUL TIPS

Except for the 4 ingredients replacing flour, all the ingredients in these recipes are things that most people have in their kitchen. Once you buy the four flour substitutes, ground almonds, coconut flour, ground flax and pysllium you will be ready to start baking all of the healthy recipes in this book.

### General Tip #1
Something you may notice when making up the batter for some recipes is that it seems wetter, that is the way it should be.

### General Tip #2
The oven temperature will be set lower than usual because of the high moisture content as mentioned in General Tip #1

## GROUND ALMONDS:
1. You can use either the raw or blanched ground almonds.
2. I specify when I want the blanched used for the looks.
3. The raw almonds will have more fiber because the skin is still on but both work equally well in all recipes.
4. Ground almonds can be found in most bulk stores and it does come prepackaged in the blanched.

## COCONUT FLOUR:
1. Coconut flour can be found in most bulk stores in bulk or prepackaged.

## GROUND FLAX:
1. You can find it in seed form and grind it yourself in a coffee grinder or use a Magic Bullet™ with the #2 blade attachment.
2. You can also find it already ground in bulk and prepackaged at most bulk stores.
3. Flax comes in golden and brown, either work fine but in some recipes I do specify golden for the looks.

## PSYLLIUM:
1. Pysllium can be found in most bulk stores in bulk.
2. Some companies have it prepackaged but don't buy the powder form, use only the pysllium husks.

**BUCKWHEAT FLOUR:**
1. Buckwheat flour is not a grain but comes from the rhubarb family.

**OILS:**
1. In the recipes that call for oil, I haven't always specified which one to use.
2. I like to use safflower oil as it is light and has very little taste so it doesn't carry into the flavoring of the product. You can use coconut oil or another oil of your choice.

**SUGAR:**
1. I have used granulated white, brown, organic palm and xylitol in all the recipes with good results.
2. Xylitol is the only one that should be used if you are diabetic and it can be found in some health food and bulk stores or purchased on line.
3. Xyla™ is the name brand that I used which can be used in place of sugar cup for cup. I was very happy with the results and no one knew the difference.
4. Palm sugar is another good sugar substitute that is low on the glycemic index and can be used cup for cup. It can also be purchased in bulk stores in either prepackaged or bulk form.

**EGGS:**
1. If you are allergic to eggs the following is a good substitute.
2. This is equivalent to 1 egg.
   - 1 tbsp ground flax + 3 tbsp water
   - Let sit for 5 minutes then beat with a fork. It will have the same consistency of an egg.

**BUTTERMILK:**
1. I use dry buttermilk powder that you add to water.
2. You can also use regular or almond milk by adding 1 tbsp vinegar for every 1 cup of milk as a substitute.
3. You can also use fresh buttermilk.

**SALT:**
1. 1 omitted salt from most of my recipes because of the growing concern of too much sodium in our diets. If you wish to add salt to any of the recipes you certainly can but I would recommend using a better salt such as unprocessed sea salt or Himalayan salt.

# Table of Contents

## MUFFINS

## CAKES

## DESSERTS

## COOKIES AND SQUARES

## OTHER GOOD STUFF

# NO BRAN BRAN MUFFINS

**WET**

- ¼ cup oil
- 2 large eggs
- ⅓ cup brown sugar, palm sugar or xylitol (Xyla ™)
- 2 tbsp molasses (fancy)
- 1½ cups buttermilk or sour milk

**DRY**

- ¾ cup ground almonds
- ⅓ cup coconut flour (sifted)
- ½ cup ground flax
- ½ cup pysllium
- 2 tsp baking powder
- ½ tsp baking soda
- ½ cup chopped nuts (your choice)
- ½ cup dried fruit (your choice)
- ½ cup semi- sweet chocolate chips

Grease a muffin pan or line with paper liners. Preheat oven to 325F.

In a large bowl whisk oil, eggs, brown sugar and molasses. Add buttermilk, whisk again.

In a medium bowl stir dry ingredients together. Add dry ingredients to wet and stir just until moist and smooth.

Spoon batter into muffin pan. Bake in preheated oven for 30-35 minutes. Remove muffins from oven and cool 10-15 minutes on wire rack. Remove muffins from pan to finish cooling on rack.

Makes 12 muffins.

Photo (opposite)

*Health Tip: 1 oz. (23) almonds per day with other heart healthy foods will reduce LDL.*

*No Bran Bran Muffins (opposite) and Pineapple Pecan Muffins (pg. 20)*

# PUMPKIN MUFFINS

**WET**

- ¼ cup of oil
- 2 large eggs
- ¼ cup molasses (fancy)
- ⅓ cup brown sugar, palm sugar or xylitol (Xyla™)
- ½ cup buttermilk or sour milk
- 1 cup pure pumpkin

**DRY**

- 1 cup ground almonds
- ½ cup coconut flour (sifted)
- ¼ cup ground flax
- ¼ cup pysllium
- 2 tsp baking powder
- ½ tsp baking soda
- 1 tsp cinnamon
- ½ tsp nutmeg
- ½ cup chopped walnuts
- ½ cup dried cranberries

Grease a muffin pan or line with paper liners. Preheat oven to 325F.

In a large bowl whisk oil, eggs, molasses and brown sugar. Add pumpkin and whisk then add buttermilk and continue whisking.
In medium bowl stir all dry ingredients together. Add dry ingredients to wet and stir just until moist and smooth.

Spoon batter into muffin pan. Bake in preheated oven 35-40 minutes. Remove muffins from oven and cool 10-15 minutes on wire rack. Remove from pan to finish cooling. Makes 12 muffins

# BANANA MUFFINS

**WET**

- ¼ cup oil
- 2 large eggs
- ¼ cup brown sugar, palm sugar or xylitol (Xyla™)
- 1 cup mashed banana
- ⅓ cup plain yogurt or sour cream
- 2 tsp vanilla
- ½ cup buttermilk or sour milk

**DRY**

- 1 cup ground almonds
- ½ cup coconut flour (sifted)
- ¼ cup ground flax
- ¼ cup pysllium
- 2 tsp baking powder
- ½ tsp baking soda
- ½ cup chopped walnuts
- ½ cup semi-sweet chocolate chips

Grease a muffin pan or line with paper liners. Preheat oven to 325F.

In large bowl whisk oil, eggs and sugar. Add mashed banana and yogurt and whisk until mixed. Add buttermilk and vanilla and continue to whisk until well mixed.

In a medium bowl stir dry ingredients together. Add dry ingredients to wet and stir just until moist and smooth.

Spoon batter into muffin pan. Bake in preheated oven 35-40 minutes. Remove muffins from oven and cool 10-15 minutes on wire rack. Remove muffins from pan to finish cooling on rack.

Makes 12 muffins.

*Health Tip: Psyllium husks are a partially fermented dietary fiber from Plantago Ovata, which helps to normalize bowel function by absorbing excess water in the intestine.*

# SEEDY NUTN' HONEY MUFFINS

**WET**

- ⅓ cup oil
- 1 large egg
- ⅓ cup brown sugar, palm sugar or xylitol (Xyla™)
- ¼ cup honey
- 1½ cups buttermilk or sour milk

**DRY**

- 1 cup ground almonds
- ⅓ cup coconut flour (sifted)
- ⅓ cup ground flax
- ⅓ cup psyllium
- 1½ tsp baking powder
- ½ tsp baking soda
- ⅓ cup chopped nuts of your choice
- 2 tbsp of each raw sunflower seeds, sesame seeds, poppy seeds and hemp seeds

Grease a muffin pan or line with paper liners. Preheat oven to 325F.

In large bowl whisk oil, egg, brown sugar and honey. Add buttermilk and continue to whisk until mixed.

In medium bowl stir dry ingredients together. Add dry ingredients to wet and mix until batter is moist and smooth.

Spoon batter into muffin pan. Bake in pre-heated oven 30-35 minutes. Remove muffins from oven and cool for 10-15 minutes on wire rack. Remove muffins from pan to finish cooling on rack.
Makes 12 muffins

*Health Tip: Coconut flour is a naturally low-carb, high fibre food ideally suited for low- carb diets.*

*Seedy Nutn' Honey Muffins pg. 12*

# CARROT MUFFINS

**WET**
- ¼ cup melted butter
- 1 large egg
- ¼ cup brown sugar, palm sugar or Xylitol (Xyla™)
- 2 tbsp molasses (fancy)
- 1½ cups buttermilk or sour milk

**DRY**
- 1 cup ground almonds
- ⅓ cup coconut flour (sifted)
- ⅓ cup ground flax
- ⅓ cup pysllium
- 1 tbsp baking powder
- ½ tsp cinnamon
- ¼ tsp nutmeg
- 1 cup grated carrots
- ½ cup chopped nuts
- ½ cup dried fruit (cranberries, raisins)

Grease a muffin pan or line with paper liners. Preheat oven to 325F.

In large bowl whisk melted butter, egg, brown sugar and molasses. Add buttermilk and whisk until mixed.

In medium bowl stir dry ingredients together. Add dry ingredients to wet and stir until batter is moist and smooth..

Spoon batter into muffin pan. Bake in preheated oven 30-35 minutes. Remove muffins from oven to cool for 10- 15 minutes on wire rack. Remove muffins from pan to finish cooling on rack.

Makes 12 muffins

*Health Tip: Flax is low in carbohydrates and high in healthy fat and fibre, which makes it a great food for weight loss*

# COCOA CHIP MUFFINS

**WET**

- ½ cup melted butter
- 2 large eggs
- ½ cup brown sugar, palm sugar or xylitol (Xyla™)
- 1½ cups buttermilk or sour milk
- 1 tsp vanilla

**DRY**

- ¾ cup ground almonds
- ⅓ cup coconut flour (sifted)
- ¼ cup ground flax
- ¼ cup psyllium
- ⅓ cup cocoa
- 1 tbsp baking powder
- ½ cup chopped nuts
- ½ cup chocolate chips
- ½ cup dried cherries (optional)*

Grease a muffin pan or use paper liners. Preheat oven to 325F

In a large bowl whisk melted butter, eggs and brown sugar. Add buttermilk and vanilla and whisk until mixed.

In a medium bowl stir dry ingredients together. Add dry ingredients to wet and mix until batter is moist and smooth.

Spoon batter into muffin pan. Bake in preheated oven 30-35 minutes. Remove muffins from oven and cool for 10-15 minutes on wire rack. Remove muffins from pan to finish cooling one rack.

*If using dried cherries it is a good idea to cut them up.

*Health Tip: Cherries are high in beta carotene, containing 19 times more than blueberries or strawberries.*

# BLUEBERRY MUFFINS

**WET**

- ¼ cup oil
- 2 large eggs
- ¼ cup brown sugar, palm sugar or xylitol (Xyla™)
- ¼ cup honey
- 1 ½ cups buttermilk or sour milk
- 1 tsp vanilla

**DRY**

- 1 cup ground almonds (blanched)
- ½ cup coconut flour (sifted)
- ¼ cup ground flax (golden)
- ¼ cup pysllium
- 2 tsp baking powder
- 1½ tsp cinnamon
- 1 cup frozen or fresh blueberries*
- ⅓ cup sliced blanched almonds (optional)

Grease a muffin pan or line with paper liners. Preheat oven to 325F. In large bowl whisk oil, eggs, brown sugar and honey. Add buttermilk and vanilla and continue whisking until mixed.
 In a medium bowl stir dry ingredients together. Add dry ingredients to wet and stir until moist and smooth. Fold in blueberries. Spoon batter into muffin pan. Bake in preheated oven for 30-35 minutes. Remove muffins from oven and cool for 10-15 minutes on wire rack. Remove from pan and finish cooling on rack. Makes 12 muffins. *If using frozen berries do not thaw.

# APPLE CRANBERRY SPICE MUFFINS

**WET**

- ¼ cup oil
- ½ cup brown sugar, palm sugar or xylitol (Xyla™)
- 2 large eggs
- 1 cup buttermilk or sour milk

**DRY**

- 1 cup ground almonds (blanched)
- ⅓ cup coconut flour (sifted)
- ⅓ cup ground flax (golden)
- ⅓ cup psyllium
- 1 tbsp baking powder
- 2 tsp cinnamon
- ½ tsp each nutmeg and ginger
- ¾ cup heaping chopped apple
- ⅔ cup dried cranberries

**TOPPING**

- 2 tsp brown sugar or palm sugar
- 1 tsp cinnamon

Grease a muffin pan or use paper liners. Preheat oven to 325F.

In large bowl whisk oil, sugar and eggs. Add buttermilk and whisk well.

In medium bowl stir all dry ingredients together except apples and cranberries. Stir in apples and cranberries until coated. Add dry ingredients to wet and stir just until moist and smooth.

Spoon batter into muffin pan. Mix topping in small bowl and sprinkle over top of batter of each muffin   Bake in oven 30-35 minutes. Remove muffins from oven and cool 10-15 minutes on wire rack. Remove muffins from pan to finish cooling on rack.

Makes 12 muffins

*Health Tip: Coconut flour contains more fibre then any whole grain.*

# ZUCCHINI CRANBERRY MUFFINS

**WET**

- ⅓ cup oil
- ⅔ cup brown sugar, palm sugar or xylitol (Xyla™)
- 2 large eggs
- 1 cup buttermilk or sour milk
- 1½ cups grated zucchini

**DRY**

- 1 cup ground almond
- ⅓ cup coconut flour (sifted)
- ⅓ cup ground flax
- ⅓ cup psyllium
- 1 tbsp baking powder
- ½ tsp baking soda
- ½ cup dried cranberries
- ½ cup chopped nuts

Grease a muffin pan or line with paper liners. Preheat oven to 325F.

In large bowl whisk oil, sugar and eggs. Whisk in buttermilk. Stir in grated zucchini.

In medium bowl stir all dry ingredients together. Add dry ingredients to wet and stir until moist and smooth.

Spoon batter into muffin pan. Bake in preheated oven 30-35 minutes. Remove muffins from oven and cool 10-15 minutes on metal cooling rack. Remove from pan to finish cooling.

Makes 12 muffins

*Health Tip: Coconut flour has a low available carbohydrate content, which can help prevent blood sugar spikes and maintain blood sugar levels after eating.*

*Zucchini Cranberry Muffins pg. 18*

# PINEAPPLE PECAN MUFFINS

**WET**

- 1 cup boiling water
- 1 cup dried pineapple

➢

- ½ cup butter softened
- ⅓ cup brown sugar, palm sugar or xylitol (Xyla™)
- 2 large eggs
- 1 ½ cups buttermilk or sour milk
- 1 tsp vanilla

**DRY**

- 1 cup ground almonds (blanched)
- ⅓ cup coconut flour (sifted)
- ⅓ cup ground flax (golden)
- ⅓ cup psyllium
- 1 tbsp. baking powder
- 1 tsp each cinnamon and ginger
- ½ cup chopped pecans

Grease a muffin pan or line with paper liners. Preheat oven to 325F.

Cut dried pineapple in pieces if they are large. In one cup glass measuring cup add dried pineapple then pour boiling water over and let sit while preparing the rest of the batter.

In large bowl cream butter and brown sugar. Add eggs one at a time. Stir in buttermilk and vanilla. It will not completely mix in. Drain pineapple and add to wet mixture.

In medium bowl stir together all dry ingredients. Add dry ingredients to wet and stir until moist and smooth.

Spoon batter into muffin pan. Bake in preheated oven for 30-35 minutes. Remove muffins from oven and cool 10-15 minutes on wire rack. Remove muffins from pan to finish cooling.

Makes 12 muffins

*Health Tip: Flax contains high levels of lignans, which are natural compounds that help prevent many types of cancers e.g. breast, colon, and prostate.*

# MOCHA NUT MUFFINS

**WET**

- ⅓ cup melted butter
- 2 large eggs
- ½ cup brown sugar, palm sugar or xylitol (Xyla™)
- 1½ cups buttermilk or sour milk
- 1 tsp vanilla

**DRY**

- 1 cup ground almonds
- ½ cup coconut flour (sifted)
- ¼ cup ground flax
- ¼ cup psyllium
- 2 tsp baking powder
- ½ tsp baking soda
- 1 tsp cinnamon
- 2 tbsp instant coffee granules
- ½ cup chopped nuts
- ½ cup semi sweet chocolate chips

Grease a muffin pan or use paper liners. Preheat oven to 325F.

In large bowl whisk melted butter, eggs and brown sugar. Add buttermilk and vanilla and continue whisking until mixed.

In medium bowl stir dry ingredients together. Add dry ingredients to wet and stir until moist and smooth.

Spoon batter into muffin pan. Bake in preheated oven 30-35 minutes. Remove muffins from oven and cool 10-15 minutes on wire rack. Remove from pan to finish cooling on rack

Makes 12 muffins

*Health Tip: Psyllium husks appear to be one of the most effective soluble fibres that significantly lower LDL cholesterol concentration.*

# LEMON POPPY SEED MUFFINS

**WET**

- ⅓ cup oil
- 1 large egg
- ½ cup white sugar or xylitol (Xyla™)
- 1 cup buttermilk or sour milk
- ½ cup sour cream
- 1 ½ tsp lemon extract
- zest from 1 lemon

**DRY**

- 1 cup ground almonds (blanched)
- ⅓ cup coconut flour (sifted)
- ⅓ cup ground flax seed (golden)
- ⅓ cup psyllium
- 2 tsp baking powder
- ½ tsp baking soda
- 3 tbsp poppy seeds

Grease a muffin pan or use paper liners. Preheat oven to 325F.

In large bowl whisk oil, egg and sugar. Whisk buttermilk and sour cream together in measuring cup and add to oil mixture. Add lemon extract and zest from lemon and whisk until well mixed.

In medium bowl stir together all dry ingredients. Add dry ingredients to wet and stir until batter is moist and smooth.

Spoon batter into muffin pan. Bake in preheated oven 30-35 minutes. Remove muffins from oven and cool 10-15 minutes on wire rack. Remove from pan to finish cooling on rack.

Makes 12 muffins

*Health Tip: Psyllium can help stabilize levels of glucose (sugar) in the blood, which may control food cravings.*

# CHOCOLATE STRUESEL CAKE

**WET**

- ¾ cup softened butter
- ⅔ cup white sugar or xylitol (Xyla™)
- 2 large eggs
- 1 tsp vanilla

- ½ cup buttermilk or sour milk
- ½ cup sour cream

**DRY**

- 1 cup ground almonds (blanched)
- ½ cup coconut flour (sifted)
- ¼ cup ground flax (golden)
- ¼ cup psyllium
- 2 tsp baking powder
- ½ tsp baking soda

**STRUESEL**

- ⅓ cup brown sugar or palm sugar
- 1 tbsp unsweetened cocoa (sifted)
- ½ cup chopped walnuts
- ¼ cup semi-sweet chocolate chips

Grease a 9 X 9 baking pan. Preheat oven to 325F.
In a large bowl cream butter and sugar with electric mixer until light and fluffy. Add eggs one at a time mixing well after each addition. Stir in vanilla.
Whisk buttermilk and sour cream together and reserve.

In medium bowl stir all dry ingredients together. To the butter and sugar mixture add dry ingredients alternating with buttermilk, sour cream mixture beginning and ending with dry. Make 3 additions of dry and 2 of wet stirring well after each addition.

Spread half the batter in prepared pan. In a small bowl mix all streusel ingredients together except chocolate chips. Sprinkle ½ the streusel mixture over batter. With the remaining batter drop spoonfuls into pan spreading evenly with a butter knife. Add chocolate chips to remaining streusel then sprinkle over top.
Bake in preheated oven 35-40 minutes. Cool on wire rack.

*Health Tip: Walnuts are an excellent source of Omega-3 fatty acids, an essential fat our body cannot produce.*

# BANANA COFFEE CAKE

**WET**

- ½ cup softened butter
- ½ cup brown sugar, palm sugar or xylitol (Xyla™)
- 2 large eggs
- 1 cup mashed banana
- 1 tsp vanilla

- ½ cup buttermilk or sour milk
- ½ cup sour cream

**DRY**

- 1 cup ground almonds (blanched)
- ⅔ cup coconut flour (sifted)
- 3 tbsp ground flax (golden)
- 2 tbsp psyllium
- 2 tsp baking powder
- ½ tsp baking soda

**TOPPING**

- 2 tbsp brown sugar or palm sugar
- 1 tsp cinnamon
- ½ cup chocolate chips
- ¼ cup chopped walnuts

Grease a 9 X 9 baking pan. Preheat oven to 325F.

In a large bowl cream butter and sugar with electric mixer until light and fluffy. Add eggs one at a time mixing well after each addition. Stir in banana and vanilla.

Whisk buttermilk and sour cream together and reserve.

In medium bowl stir all dry ingredients together. To the banana mixture add dry ingredients alternating with buttermilk, sour cream mixture, beginning and ending with dry. Make 3 additions of dry and 2 of wet stirring well after each addition. Spread batter in prepared baking pan.

In a small bowl mix all topping ingredients. Sprinkle over batter.

Bake in preheated oven 40-45 minutes. Cool on wire rack.

*Banana Coffee Cake (left) pg. 24 & Chocolate Streusel Cake (right) pg. 23*

# APPLE SKOR CAKE

**WET**
- ¼ cup softened butter
- ½ cup white sugar or xylitol (Xyla™)
- 2 large eggs
- 1 tsp vanilla
- ½ cup buttermilk or sour milk
- ½ cup sour cream

**DRY**
- 1 cup ground almonds
- ½ cup coconut flour (sifted)
- 3 tbsp ground flax
- 2 tbsp psyllium
- 1½ tsp baking powder
- ½ tsp baking soda
- 6 tbsp Skor toffee bit
- ¾ cup finely chopped apples

**TOPPING**
- 2 tbsp brown sugar or palm sugar
- 6 tbsp Skor toffee bits
- ½ tsp cinnamon
- ⅓ cup chocolate chips

Grease a 9 X 9 baking pan. Preheat oven to 325F.

In a large bowl cream butter and sugar with electric mixer on high, mix until light and fluffy. Add eggs one at a time mixing well after each addition. Stir in vanilla. Whisk buttermilk and sour cream together and reserve.

In a medium bowl stir all dry ingredients together including the toffee bits. To butter, sugar mixture add dry ingredients alternating with buttermilk, sour cream mixture, beginning and ending with dry. Make 3 additions of dry and 2 of wet stirring well after each addition. Fold in apples. Spread batter in prepared pan. In a small bowl mix all topping ingredients. Sprinkle over top of batter. Bake in preheated oven 40-45 minutes. Cool on wire rack.

# HAWAIIAN CAKE

**WET**

- ½ cup oil
- ¾ cup white sugar or xylitol (Xyla™)
- 2 large eggs
- ¾ cup mashed banana
- ¾ cup un-drained crushed pineapple
- 1½ tsp vanilla
- ½ cup buttermilk or sour milk

**DRY**

- 1 cup ground almonds
- ¾ cup coconut flour (sifted)
- ¼ cup ground flax
- ¼ cup psyllium
- 1 tbsp baking powder
- ½ tsp baking soda

**TOPPING**

- ½ cup chopped nuts
- ¼ cup brown sugar or palm sugar
- 1 tsp nutmeg
- ½ cup unsweetened flaked or shredded coconut

Grease a 9 X 9 baking pan. Preheat oven to 325F.

In large bowl whisk oil, sugar and eggs together. Add banana, crushed pineapple and vanilla and whisk until well mixed.

In medium bowl mix all dry ingredients together. Add to the pineapple mixture the dry ingredients alternating with buttermilk beginning and ending with dry. Make 2 additions of dry and 1 of wet stirring well after each addition. Spread the batter in prepared pan.

In small bowl mix all topping ingredients and sprinkle over batter.

Bake in preheated oven 45-50 minutes. Cool on wire rack.

*Health Tip: Almonds are the most nutrient dense tree nuts. They are an excellent source of vitamins B12, E and magnesium.*

# CARROT CAKE

**WET**

- ½ cup oil
- ½ cup brown sugar, palm sugar or xylitol (Xyla™)
- ¼ cup molasses (fancy)
- 2 large eggs
- 1 tsp vanilla
- ¾ cup buttermilk or sour milk
- 1½ cups grated carrot

**DRY**

- 1 cup ground almonds
- ½ cup coconut flour (sifted)
- ¼ cup ground flax
- ¼ cup psyllium
- 1½ tsp baking powder
- ¾ tsp baking soda
- 1½ tsp cinnamon
- ½ tsp nutmeg
- ½ tsp ginger
- ½ cup chopped nuts

**ICING**

- ½ package cream cheese softened
- 1 tbsp butter softened
- ¼ cup honey
- ½ tsp vanilla

Grease a 9 X 9 baking pan. Preheat oven to 325F.

In large bowl whisk oil, sugar, molasses and eggs. Add vanilla and buttermilk and whisk again. Stir in grated carrots.

In medium bowl stir all dry ingredients together. Add dry ingredients to wet and stir until moist and smooth. Spread in prepared pan. Bake in preheated oven 30-35 minutes. Cool on wire rack

Beat cream cheese and butter together. Add honey and vanilla and beat until smooth and creamy. When cake is cooled spread icing over top.

*Carrot Cake (opposite)*

# PUMPKIN SPICE CAKE

**WET**
- ½ cup softened butter
- 2/3 cup brown sugar, palm sugar or xylitol (Xyla™)
- 2 large eggs
- 1 cup pure pumpkin
- ½ cup orange juice
- ¼ cup buttermilk or sour milk
- ½ cup sour cream

**DRY**
- 1 cup ground almonds
- ¾ cup coconut flour(sifted)
- 2 tbsp ground flax
- 2 tbsp psyllium
- 1 tbsp baking powder
- ½ tsp baking soda
- 1½ tsp cinnamon
- ½ tsp ginger and nutmeg
- ½ orange zest
- ½ cup raisins

**TOPPING**
- 2 tbsp brown sugar or palm sugar
- ½ cup chopped nuts
- 1 tsp cinnamon


Grease a 9 X 9 baking pan. Preheat oven o 325F.
In large bowl cream butter and sugar with an electric mixer until light and fluffy. Add eggs one at a time mixing well after each addition. Stir in pumpkin and orange juice. Whisk buttermilk and sour cream together and reserve.

In a medium bowl stir all dry ingredients together. To pumpkin mixture add dry ingredients alternately with buttermilk, sour cream mixture beginning and ending with dry. Make 3 additions of dry and 2 of wet, mixing well after each addition. Spread batter in prepared pan.

In a small bowl mix all topping ingredients together. Sprinkle topping over batter.
Bake in preheated oven 45-50 minutes. Cool on wire rack.

# MOCHA PECAN CAKE

## WET
- ¾ cup softened butter
- ⅔ cup brown sugar, palm sugar or xylitol (Xyla™)
- 2 large eggs
- 1 tsp vanilla
- 2 tbsp instant coffee granules
- 2 tbsp warm water
- ½ cup sour cream
- ½ cup buttermilk or sour milk

## DRY
- 1 cup ground almonds
- ½ cup coconut flour (sifted)
- ¼ cup ground flax
- ¼ cup psyllium
- 2 tsp baking powder
- ½ tsp baking soda

## TOPPING
- 2 tbsp brown sugar or palm sugar
- ½ cup chocolate chips
- ½ cup chopped pecans
- 1 tsp cinnamon
- 1 tsp instant coffee
- ½ tsp baking soda

Grease a 9 X 9 baking pan. Preheat oven to 325F.

In large bowl cream butter and sugar with an electric mixer until light and fluffy. Add eggs one at a time mixing well after each addition. Combine instant coffee granules and warm water. On low speed of mixer add coffee water mixture, vanilla and mix.

Whisk sour cream and buttermilk together and reserve.

In a medium bowl stir all dry ingredients together. To coffee mixture add dry ingredients alternating with buttermilk, sour cream mixture beginning and ending with dry. Make 4 additions of dry and 3 of wet mixing well after each addition. Spread batter in prepared pan.

In a small bowl mix all topping ingredients together. Sprinkle topping over batter. Bake in preheated oven 40-45 minutes. Cool on wire rack.

# CHOCOLATE ZUCCHINI CAKE

**WET**

- ¾ cup softened butter
- ⅔ cup brown sugar, palm sugar or xylitol (Xyla™)
- 2 large eggs
- 1 tsp vanilla
- 1 cup grated zucchini
- ¾ sour cream
- ½ cup buttermilk or sour milk

**DRY**

- 1 cup ground almonds
- ½ cup coconut flour (sifted)
- ¼ cup ground flax
- ¼ cup psyllium
- 1½ tsp baking powder
- ¾ tsp baking soda
- ½ cup unsweetened cocoa (sifted)

| TOPPING | OR | ICING |
|---|---|---|
| 2 tbsp brown sugar or palm sugar | | 8 oz. cream cheese |
| ½ cup chocolate chips | | ⅓ cup honey |
| ½ cup chopped nuts | | 4 tbsp cocoa |

Grease a 9 X 9 baking pan or 8" spring form pan. Preheat oven to 325F.

In a large bowl cream butter and sugar with electric mixer until light and fluffy. Add eggs one at a time mixing well after each addition. Stir in vanilla and grated zucchini.

Whisk sour cream and buttermilk together and reserve.

In medium bowl stir all dry ingredients together. To the zucchini mixture add dry ingredients alternately with sour cream, buttermilk mixture beginning and ending with dry. Make 4 additions of dry and 3 of wet, mixing well after each addition. Scrape sides of bowl after stirring in each addition. Spread batter in prepared pan of your choice. If using 9 x 9 square pan sprinkle with topping. Bake in preheated oven 45-50 minutes. Cool on wire rack.

If using a spring form pan, bake cake according to directions then cool. Beat cream cheese, honey and cocoa with electric mixer until smooth. Place cooled cake on plate and spread with icing.

*Chocolate Zucchini Cake (opposite)*

# ORANGE POPPY SEED CAKE

**WET**
- ¾ cup butter softened
- ½ cup brown sugar, palm sugar or xylitol (Xyla™)
- 4 large eggs
- ½ tsp vanilla
- 1 cup buttermilk or sour milk
- 1 large orange (grate orange then juice)

**DRY**
- 1 cup blanched ground almonds
- ½ cup coconut flour (sifted)
- ¼ cup ground flax (golden)
- ¼ cup psyllium
- 1 tbsp baking powder
- ⅓ cup poppy seeds

**GLAZE**

¼ cup orange juice (either fresh or frozen)
2 tbsp honey

Grease a 9 X 9 cake pan. Preheat oven to 325F.
In large bowl cream butter and sugar until light and fluffy. Add eggs one at a time mixing well after each addition. Stir in vanilla, buttermilk, orange juice and grated orange peel.

In medium bowl stir all dry ingredients together. Add dry to wet and mix until moist and smooth. Pour batter into prepared pan. Bake in oven 40-45 minutes. Remove from oven and let cool on cooling rack.

While cake is cooling, mix glaze ingredients together in small pan on stove. Using a toothpick poke holes in top of cake and pour glaze over. ( photo pg. 53)

*Health Tip: The poppy seed's unique nutty aromatic flavor is because of many fatty acids and essential volatile oils, which comprise about 50% of net weight. The seeds are especially rich in oleic and linoleic acids. Oleic acid, a mono-unsaturated fatty acid, helps lower LDL or "bad cholesterol" and increase HDL or "good cholesterol" levels in the blood. Research studies suggest that the Mediterranean diet which is rich in monounsaturated fatty acids helps to prevent coronary artery disease and strokes by favoring healthy blood lipid profile.*

# CHOCOLATE CHEESECAKE

**BASE**

- 1 ⅓ cup ground almonds
- 2 tbsp unsweetened cocoa powder (sifted)
- 1½ tbsp brown sugar, palm sugar or xylitol (Xyla™)
- ½ cup melted butter

**FILLING**

- 2 packages cream cheese (softened)
- ⅓ cup white sugar, palm sugar or xylitol (Xyla™)
- 1 envelope unflavored gelatin (2 ½ tsp)
- ½ cup cold water
- 4 squares semi sweet chocolate, melted
- ½ cup whipping cream, whipped

**TOPPING**

- ½ cup whipping cream, whipped
- grated chocolate (garnish)
- ⅓ cup toasted sliced almonds (garnish)

Preheat oven to 325F.

In medium bowl mix ground almonds, cocoa powder and sugar. Add melted butter and stir until mixed. Press into 9"spring form pan. Bake in oven 15 minutes. Remove and let cool. Leave ring on.

In large bowl with an electric mixer beat cream cheese until smooth, beat in sugar. Set aside. In small saucepan add water and sprinkle gelatin over. Let sit 5 minutes. Stir over low heat until gelatin dissolves. On low speed of mixer, blend warm gelatin mixture into cream cheese. Beat in melted chocolate. Fold in whipped cream. Pour over cooled crust and refrigerate 4 hours. Remove ring from pan.

Spread with whipped cream and garnish with grated chocolate and sliced almonds.

Serves 10

*Health Tip: Chocolate contains many of the benefits of dark vegetables. These benefits are from flavonoids, which act as antioxidants protecting the body from aging. Dark chocolate offers the highest amount of flavonoids.*

### CHOCOLATE BASE
- ½ cup butter
- 3 squares unsweetened chocolate
- ⅔ cup white sugar, palm sugar or xylitol (Xyla™)
- 1 tsp vanilla
- 3 eggs
- ¼ cup milk

➤
- ⅓ cup ground almonds
- ¼ cup coconut flour (sifted)
- 1 tbsp ground flax
- 1 tbsp psyllium
- 1½ tsp baking powder

Grease a 9" spring form pan. Preheat oven to 325F.
In medium saucepan melt butter and chocolate on low heat, stirring until smooth. Remove from heat and pour into medium bowl. Add sugar, vanilla and eggs. Whisk well. Add milk and whisk. In small bowl stir all dry ingredients together. Add to chocolate mixture and stir until batter is smooth and well blended. Spread into prepared pan. Bake in oven for 25-30 minutes. Cool on wire rack.

### FILLING
- 2 cups fresh strawberries
- 1 package gelatin (2½ tsp)
- ⅓ cup white sugar or xylitol (Xyla™)
- 2 tbsp lemon juice
- 1¼ cup whipping cream
- 1½ cups sliced strawberries

➤
- ¾ cup whipping cream

Mash the 2 cups of strawberries and put in 2 cup measuring cup and add water to make 1¼ cups.
In large saucepan combine gelatin and sugar, stir in strawberry liquid and lemon juice. Bring mixture to a boil stirring constantly to dissolve sugar and gelatin. Remove from heat and pour into large bowl. Refrigerate until starting to set (this could take 1 hr).

Beat 1¼ cups whipping cream to form stiff peaks. Reserve. Remove strawberry mixture from refrigerator. Beat on high speed of electric mixer until light. Fold in whipped cream. Fold in sliced strawberries. Spread over chocolate base with the ring still on.

Chill until set (this could take 1½ hrs). Remove ring and leave in refrigerator until ready to serve.

When ready to serve beat ¾ cup whipping cream to form stiff peaks. Add 2 tsp sugar and 1 tsp vanilla and stir. Spread over top of filling. Garnish with grated chocolate, sliced strawberries and/or sliced almonds. Serves 10

ALTERNATIVE: Fresh raspberries or peaches can be used in place of strawberries when fruit is in season.

*Strawberry Mousse Cake*

# PEACH TRIFLE

## POUND CAKE

- ¾ cup softened butter
- ¾ cup white sugar or xylitol (Xyla™)
- 2 large eggs
- ½ cup buttermilk or sour milk
- 1 tsp vanilla

➢
- 1 cup ground almonds (blanched)
- ¾ cup coconut flour (sifted)
- 2 tbsp ground flax (golden)
- 2 tbsp psyllium
- 2 tsp baking powder

Grease a 9 x 9 baking pan. Preheat oven to 325F.
In large bowl cream butter and sugar. Add eggs one at a time beating well after each addition. Beat mixture until light and fluffy. Stir buttermilk and vanilla together and set aside.

In medium bowl stir all dry ingredients together. To butter mixture add dry ingredients alternating with wet, beginning and ending with dry, making 3 additions of dry and 2 of wet. Pour batter into prepared pan and bake 25-30 minutes. Remove from oven and cool on wire rack.

## CUSTARD

- 6 eggs
- ⅔ cup white sugar or xylitol (Xyla™)
- 3 tbsp potato starch
- 2 cans coconut milk plus enough milk to equal 4 cups
- 1 tbsp vanilla

➢
- 6-8 medium peaches peeled and sliced
- brandy or sherry (optional)
- 1 cup whipping cream whipped

In large bowl beat eggs and sugar until foamy. Whisk in potato starch then gradually stir in coconut milk. Pour into large pot and cook over low heat stirring constantly until thickened, approximately 10-15 minutes. Stir in vanilla. Cool slightly.

To assemble trifle, use a large bowl and pour some of the custard to cover bottom. Cut the cake into chunks and spread over custard. If using brandy pour some over cake.  Put fresh peaches on top. Repeat the process ending with custard. Let set in refrigerator for 2 hrs. Before serving spread whipped cream over top and garnish with grated chocolate and or toasted sliced almonds.

ALTERNATIVE: Use fresh strawberries or raspberries in place of peaches.

*Peach Trifle*

# CHERRY COBBLER

**FILLING**
- 6 cups frozen cherries or frozen fruit of your choice
- 3 tbsp potato starch
- ½ cup white sugar, palm sugar or xylitol (Xyla™)
- 1 tsp cinnamon

**TOPPING**
- ¾ cup ground almonds
- ¼ cup coconut flour (sifted)
- 2 tbsp ground flax
- 2 tbsp psyllium
- 2 tbsp sugar
- 1 tbsp baking powder
- ¼ tsp salt
- ⅓ cup cold butter
- 1 large egg
- ¾ cup buttermilk or sour milk

Preheat oven to 375F.

Combine cherries, potato starch, sugar and cinnamon in a 2.5L casserole dish or 8 X 8 glass pan. Bake in oven 30 minutes. Meanwhile combine all dry ingredients in a medium bowl. Using a pastry cutter, cut butter into dry ingredients. Whisk egg and buttermilk together. Add to dry ingredients and stir until mixed. After 30 minutes of baking remove cherries from oven and spoon batter on top making 6 biscuits. Bake another 30 minutes. Serve warm.

# PEANUT BUTTER COOKIES

**WET**

- 1 cup softened butter
- 1½ cups natural no sugar added peanut butter
- ⅔ cup brown sugar, palm sugar or xylitol (Xyla™)
- 2 tbsp honey
- 2 large eggs
- 1 tsp vanilla

**DRY**

- 1 cup ground almonds
- ¼ cup ground flax
- ¼ cup coconut flour (sifted)
- 2 tbsp psyllium
- 1 tsp baking powder
- 1 tsp baking soda
- ½ cup semi sweet chocolate chips

Preheat oven to 350F.
In large bowl cream butter, peanut butter, sugar and honey together. Add eggs and beat until light and fluffy. Stir in vanilla.

In medium bowl stir all dry ingredients together except for chocolate chips. Stir dry ingredients into wet and mix until smooth. Add chocolate chips and stir just until mixed.

Using a small ice cream scoop or two tablespoons, scoop batter onto cookie sheets. With a damp fork press cookies down lightly. Bake in oven 14-15 minutes until cookies are golden brown. Remove from oven and cool slightly then remove to wire cooling rack to finish cooling. Makes 3 dozen

*Health Tip: Flax has 75 times more lignans than other plants. Lignans are phyto-estrogens that may help alleviate menopausal symptoms such as hot flashes.*

# GINGER MOLASSES COOKIES

**WET**
- ⅔ cup softened butter
- ½ cup brown sugar, palm sugar or xylitol (Xyla™)
- 2 tbsp molasses (fancy)
- 2 large eggs

**DRY**
- 1 cup ground almonds
- ½ cup coconut flour (sifted)
- ¼ cup ground flax
- 2 tbsp psyllium
- 1 tsp baking powder
- 1 tsp baking soda
- 2 tsp ginger
- 1 tsp cinnamon
- 2 tbsp crystallized ginger which has been soaked in hot water, drained then chopped

Preheat oven to 350F.

In large bowl cream butter, sugar and molasses. Add eggs and beat until light.

In medium bowl stir all dry ingredients together except crystallized ginger. Add dry ingredients to wet and stir until smooth. Stir in crystallized ginger. Take a spoonful of batter and roll in ball (optional to roll ball in white sugar) and place on cookie sheet. Press down with palm of hand.

Bake in oven 15-17 minutes or until cookies are golden brown. Remove from oven and cool slightly then remove to wire cooling rack to finish cooling. Makes 2 dozen

# DOUBLE CHOCOLATE COOKIES

**WET**

- 1 cup butter
- ¾ cup brown sugar, palm sugar or xylitol (Xyla™)
- 2 large eggs
- 1 tbsp almond or regular milk

**DRY**

- 1 cup ground almonds
- ¼ cup coconut flour (sifted)
- ¼ cup ground flax
- 2 tbsp psyllium
- ⅔ cup unsweetened cocoa powder (sifted)
- 1 tsp baking soda
- ½ cup semi sweet chocolate chips
- ½ cup chopped nuts (optional)

Preheat oven to 350F.

In large bowl cream butter and sugar. Add eggs and almond milk and beat well.

In medium bowl stir together all dry ingredients except chocolate chips and nuts.

Add dry ingredients to wet and stir until smooth. Add chocolate chips and nuts (if using) to batter and stir well.

Using a small ice cream scoop or 2 tablespoons scoop out batter on to cookie sheets. Bake in oven 12-14 minutes. Remove from oven and cool slightly then remove to wire cooling rack to finish cooling.

Makes 2 ½ dozen

(photo pg. 44)

*Health Tip: Psyllium can help with weight loss by absorbing water, making the stomach feel full longer.*

*A True Almond Cookie (pg. 43) & Double Chocolate Cookie (pg. 41)*

# A TRUE ALMOND COOKIE

**WET**

- ½ cup softened butter
- ½ cup white sugar or xylitol (Xyla™)
- 1 large egg
- ½ tsp pure almond extract

**DRY**

- 1 cup ground blanched almonds
- 5 tbsp coconut flour (sifted)
- 1 tbsp psyllium
- ½ tsp baking powder
- ¾ cup sliced blanched almonds

Preheat oven to 350F.

Cream butter and sugar. Add egg and almond extract and beat until fluffy.

In medium bowl stir all dry ingredients together except sliced almonds. Add dry ingredients to butter mixture and stir until smooth.

Take a spoonful of dough and roll it into a ball. Break up sliced almonds on a piece of waxed paper. Roll balls of dough in sliced almonds and place on cookie sheet. Flatten slightly with palm of hand.

Bake in oven 15-18 minutes or until lightly golden on top. Remove from oven and cool slightly then remove to wire cooling rack to finish cooling.

Makes 1½ - 2 dozen.
(photo pg. 44)

*Health Tip: Psyllium fibre is one of the best ways to help detoxify and maintain a clean and healthy digestive system.*

# CHOCOLATE TRAIL MIX COOKIES

**WET**

- 1 cup butter
- ½ cup brown sugar, palm sugar or xylitol (Xyla™)
- 2 large eggs
- 2 tsp vanilla

**DRY**

- ⅔ cup ground almonds
- ⅓ cup coconut flour (sifted)
- ¼ cup ground flax
- 2 tbsp psyllium
- ⅓ cup unsweetened cocoa powder (sifted)
- 1 tsp baking soda

- ½ cup raw pumpkin seeds
- ½ cup raw sunflower seeds
- ⅓ cup hemp seeds
- ½ cup semi sweet chocolate chips
- ½ cup dried cranberries
- ½ cup chopped nuts of your choice

Preheat oven to 350F.

In a large bowl cream butter and sugar together. Add eggs and vanilla and beat until fluffy.

In medium bowl stir all dry ingredients together except seeds, fruit and nuts. Add dry ingredients to butter mixture and stir well. Add all the seeds, dried fruit and nuts and stir until well mixed.

Using a small ice cream scoop or 2 tablespoons, scoop out batter onto cookie sheets. Bake in oven 14-15 minutes. Remove from oven and cool slightly then remove to wire cooling rack to finish cooling.

Makes 2½ – 3 dozen

*Health Tip: Pumpkin Seeds -great source of magnesium*
*Sunflower Seeds- great source of Vitamin E*
*Poppy Seeds- great source of B Vitamins*
*Sesame Seeds- good source of Calcium*

# PUMPKIN COOKIES

**WET**

- ¾ cup softened butter
- 2 tbsp honey
- ¼ cup brown sugar, palm sugar or xylitol (Xyla™)
- 2 large eggs
- ¾ cup pure pumpkin

**DRY**

- 1 cup ground almonds
- ⅓ cup ground flax
- ⅓ cup coconut flour (sifted)
- 2 tbsp psyllium
- 2 tsp baking powder
- ½ tsp baking soda
- 1 tsp cinnamon
- ½ cup dried cranberries
- ½ cup pumpkin seeds (raw)
- ½ cup chocolate chips

Preheat oven to 350F.
In large bowl cream butter, honey and brown sugar until light. Add eggs and beat well. Stir in pumpkin.
In medium bowl stir all dry ingredients except cranberries, pumpkin seeds and chocolate chips. Add cranberries, pumpkin seeds and chocolate chips.
Add dry ingredients to wet and stir until moist and smooth.
Using a small ice cream scoop or two tablespoons scoop batter onto cookie sheet.  Bake in oven 15-17 minutes. Remove from oven and cool slightly then remove to cooling rack to finish cooling.
Makes 2 dozen

# BISCOTTI

**WET**

- 3 large eggs
- ¼ cup melted butter
- 1 tsp vanilla

**DRY**

- 1½ cup ground almonds (blanched)
- ½ cup golden ground flax seed
- ¼ cup coconut flour (sifted)
- ¼ cup psyllium
- ⅔ cup white sugar, palm sugar or xylitol (Xyla™)
- 2 tsp baking powder
- ½ tsp each baking soda and cream of tartar
- ⅔ cup chopped raw almonds

➢
- 1 egg yolk
- 1 tbsp milk

Grease cookie sheet. Preheat oven to 350F.

In large bowl whisk all dry ingredients together except chopped almonds. Stir in chopped almonds.

Melt butter in small saucepan. In medium bowl whisk eggs and vanilla. Whisk melted butter into egg mixture. Pour egg mixture over dry ingredients and stir. Dough will be wet. Divide dough into 2 balls. Using a piece of waxed paper place one ball of dough into it and working lengthwise shape dough into a log approximately 10" long. Place on cookie sheet. Repeat with 2nd ball.

Lightly beat egg yolk and milk. Brush mixture over top of each log. Bake for 15 minutes. Remove from oven and brush with egg yolk mixture and sprinkle tops with brown sugar. Bake for another 15 minutes. Remove from oven and let sit 5-6 minutes. Slice into ¾ inch thick cookies and place cookies on 2 cookie sheets. Reduce oven to 275F and bake in oven another 30-40 minutes.

The goal is to bake until they are crunchy.

Makes 24 cookies

*Biscotti pg. 46*

# BROWNIES

**WET**

- ½ cup melted butter
- ½ cup white sugar, palm sugar or xylitol (Xyla™)
- 2 large eggs
- 1 tsp vanilla
- 1 cup buttermilk or sour milk

**DRY**

- ½ cup ground almonds
- ¼ cup coconut flour (sifted)
- 2 tbsp ground flax
- 2 tbsp psyllium
- ½ cup unsweetened cocoa
- 2 tsp baking powder
- ½ cup chocolate chips
- ½ cup chopped nuts (optional)

Grease an 8 X 8 baking pan. Preheat oven to 325F.

In large bowl whisk melted butter and sugar. Add eggs and vanilla and whisk until well blended. Stir in buttermilk.

In medium bowl stir all dry ingredients together. Add dry ingredients to wet and stir until moist and smooth. Pour batter into prepared pan.

Bake in oven 30-35 minutes. Remove from oven and cool on wire rack. Makes 16 pieces.

# PEANUT BUTTER ENERGY BARS

**WET**

- ½ cup peanut butter (no sugar, no salt added)
- ¼ cup brown sugar, palm sugar or xylitol (Xyla™)
- ¼ cup honey
- 2 tbsp oil
- 2 large eggs
- 1 tsp vanilla
- ½ cup milk (almond or regular)

**DRY**

- ¾ cup ground almonds
- ¼ cup coconut flour (sifted)
- ¼ cup ground flax
- 2 tbsp psyllium
- ½ tsp each baking powder and soda
- ½ cup chocolate chips
- ¼ cup each sliced almonds, raw sunflower seeds & pumpkin seeds
- 2 tbsp sesame or hemp seeds
- ½ cup dried cranberries

Grease a 9 X 9 baking pan. Preheat oven to 325F.

In large bowl cream peanut butter, sugar, honey and oil until blended. Add eggs and continue beating. Add vanilla and milk and stir until well mixed.

In medium bowl stir all dry ingredients together. Add dry ingredients to wet and stir until moist. Pour batter into prepared pan.

Bake in oven 30-35 minutes. Remove from oven and cool on wire rack.

# LEMON CHEESECAKE SQUARES

### BASE

- ¾ cup ground almonds
- ¼ cup coconut flour
- ¼ cup ground flax
- 1 tbsp psyllium
- 1 tbsp brown sugar, palm sugar or xylitol (Xyla™)
- ½ cup melted butter

### FILLING

- 1 package cream cheese softened
- ⅓ cup white sugar, or xylitol (Xyla™)
- 2 eggs
- ½ cup sour cream
- 2 tbsp lemon juice
- grated peel from 1 lemon

Preheat oven to 350F.

In medium bowl stir together ground almonds, coconut flour, ground flax, pysllium and sugar. Melt butter in small saucepan and pour over dry ingredients. Stir until well mixed.

Spread mixture into an 8 X 8 pan patting down firmly with the back of spoon. Bake in oven 10 minutes.

In large bowl beat cream cheese and sugar until light and fluffy. Add eggs and continue beating until well mixed. Stir in sour cream, lemon juice and lemon peel. Pour over base and return to oven to bake 35-40 minutes.

Cool on wire rack. Refrigerate until ready to serve.Cut into squares and garnish with fresh fruit and whipped cream.

Makes 24 small squares.

Note: For a 9 x 13 pan, double the recipe.

*Lemon Cheesecake Squares pg. 52 (outer) & Orange Poppy Seed Cake pg. 34 (inner)*

# GARLIC AND 3 CHEESE MUFFINS

**WET**
- ½ cup melted butter
- 2 large eggs
- 4 cloves garlic pressed
- 1¼ cups buttermilk or sour milk

**DRY**
- 1 cup blanched ground almonds
- ½ cup coconut flour (sifted)
- ⅓ cup ground flax (golden)
- ⅓ cup psyllium
- 1 tbsp baking powder
- 1 cup grated cheddar cheese
- ¼ cup parmesan cheese
- ¼ cup crumbled blue cheese

Grease a muffin pan or line with paper liners. Preheat oven to 325F.

In large bowl whisk melted butter, eggs, garlic and buttermilk.
In medium bowl stir ground almond, coconut flour, flax, psyllium and baking powder. Add cheese and stir until evenly mixed.

Add dry ingredients to wet and stir just until moist and smooth.

Spoon batter into muffin pan. Bake in preheated oven for 30-35 minutes. Remove muffins from oven and cool just enough to remove from pan.
These are so good served warm with butter.
Makes 12 muffins (photo pg. 55)

*Health Tip: Garlic is one of the most valuable foods on the planet. It may lower blood pressure, cholesterol and aids in digestion. It is a potent immune system booster and a natural antibiotic.*

# SWEET POTATO BISCUITS

**WET**
- ¾ cup cooked mashed sweet potato
- ¼ cup melted butter
- 1 cup buttermilk or sour milk
- 1 egg

**DRY**
- 1 ⅓ cup ground almond (blanched)
- ⅓ cup coconut flour
- ⅓ cup ground flax (golden)
- 2 tbsp psyllium
- 1 tbsp baking powder
- ½ tsp salt

Grease cookie sheet. Preheat oven to 375F.

In a small bowl whisk sweet potato, melted butter, buttermilk and egg.

In large bowl combine all dry ingredients. Add wet ingredients to dry ingredients and mix until just combined. Mixture will be wetter than what you expect. Using 2 tablespoons spoon batter onto baking sheet.

Bake in oven 25-30 minutes.

Makes 12 biscuits (photo pg. 57)

ALTERNATIVE: Replace sweet potato with ⅔ cup sour cream and reduce melted butter to 2 tbsp.

*Health Tip: Sweet Potatoes have a superior content of fibre compared to other potatoes. They are also rich in Vitamin A, which is helpful in the prevention of some types of cancer. They are also a great source of Vitamins C and E that are potent antioxidants.*

# RAISIN BREAD

**WET**
- 1½ cups buttermilk or sour milk
- ¼ cup oil
- 2 large eggs

**DRY**
- 1½ cup ground almonds
- ½ cup light buckwheat flour
- ½ cup flax
- ½ cup psyllium
- 1 tbsp baking powder
- 2 tbsp sugar (optional)
- ½ tsp salt
- ½ cup raisins
- 1 tsp cinnamon

Grease a 9 X 5 loaf pan. Preheat oven to 325F.

In medium bowl whisk buttermilk, oil and eggs.

In large bowl stir all dry ingredients together then add raisins and cinnamon.

Add wet ingredients to dry and stir until moist and smooth. Pour batter into loaf pan and bake in oven 1 hour. Remove from oven and turn out onto wire rack to cool.

This bread is good toasted as well as plain. Refrigerate it or I like to slice it up and freeze it.

(photo pg. 57)

ALTERNATIVE: Use any kind of dried fruit you like or omit for plain bread.

*Health Tip: Flax is a natural food that has been consumed for thousands of years with many health benefits.*

*Raisin Bread pg. 56 (upper left), Sweet Potato Biscuits pg. 55 (upper right), &*
*Garlic & 3 Cheese Muffins pg. 54 (lower left)*

# BUCKWHEAT BATTER BREAD

**WET**
- ¼ cup warm water
- 1 tsp sugar
- 1 tbsp dry active yeast
- 1 cup milk
- 2 tbsp butter
- 2 tbsp honey
- 2 eggs

**DRY**
- ¾ cup ground almond
- ¾ cup light buckwheat flour
- ¾ cup ground flax
- 2 tbsp psyllium
- 2 tbsp coconut flour (sifted)
- 1 tsp salt
- 1 tsp baking powder

Grease a 9 X 5 loaf pan. In a small bowl dissolve sugar in warm water. Sprinkle yeast over and let sit 5 minutes.

Meanwhile heat milk, honey and butter in a small pan until butter is melted. Pour milk in large bowl and whisk in yeast mixture. Whisk in eggs.

In a medium bowl stir all dry ingredients together. Add dry ingredients to wet and stir until moist and smooth. Pour batter into loaf pan, cover with a towel and place in oven with light on. Let rise 40-45 minutes. Take out of oven and heat oven to 325F. Place bread in oven and bake 40 minutes. Remove pan from oven and turn bread onto cooling rack. Slice when cooled.

*Health Tips:*
*Buckwheat is high in fiber.*
*Buckwheat lowers glucose levels and is beneficial for managing diabetes.*
*Buckwheat has been found to lower blood pressure and reduce cholesterol.*
*Buckwheat is a fruit seed and is a gluten-free alternative to grains.*

# BUCKWHEAT BLUEBERRY PANCAKES

**WET**
- 2 cups almond or regular milk
- 2 eggs
- 1 tsp vanilla

**DRY**
- ¾ cup buckwheat flour
- ¾ cup ground flax
- ½ cup ground almonds
- 1 tbsp baking powder
- 1 tbsp cinnamon
- 1 cup fresh or frozen blueberries

Heat oil in nonstick or cast iron frying pan. Whisk milk, eggs and vanilla in small bowl. Stir all dry ingredients in large bowl and add blueberries. Add wet ingredients to dry and stir until moist and smooth.

Ladle batter into nonstick or cast iron frying pan. Spread batter out a bit and cook covered for 3 minutes. Turn pancake and continue cooking for another 3 minutes. Serve warm with butter and maple syrup.

# MULTI SEED CRACKERS

*PARCHMENT PAPER REQUIRED*

**WET**
- 6 oz cold water
- 2 tbsp oil

**DRY**
- ¼ cup ground almonds
- ¼ cup light buckwheat flour
- 2 tbsp coconut flour (sifted)
- 2 tbsp psyllium
- ¼ tsp salt
- ½ cup sesame seeds
- 2 tbsp each sunflower, pumpkin, and flax seeds
- ¼ cup finely chopped walnuts

Preheat oven to 325F. Move oven rack to bottom third of oven,

Stir together all dry ingredients. Add water and oil and stir until forms a ball. Let sit while preparing parchment paper. Divide dough into 2 balls.

Cut a piece of parchment paper the size of two regular sized cookie sheets. Moisten work surface with a bit of water. Place parchment over (this keeps paper from sliding during rolling) then put ball of dough on top. Cut a piece of waxed paper the same size for over top. Roll dough out going from center to outer edges, so dough is the same thickness in the centre as the edges. The edges will not be even, not a problem. Dough should be about 1/8" thick. Peel waxed paper off and using a pizza cutter or thin bladed knife cut to cracker size. Prick each cracker in several places with the tines of a fork. Slide parchment paper with dough on it onto cookie sheet. Repeat with 2nd ball of dough.
Bake in oven for 30-35 minutes. Remove and break off any outside crackers that are crispy. Gently break up the rest of the crackers and place around pan, put back in the oven any crackers that aren't crispy and bake another 5-10 minutes or until crackers are crispy.

NOTE: You may have to take some off the pan and continue baking the rest in order for them all to get crispy. The outside crackers tend to get a little browner but they are still good.

Makes approximately 6-7 doz. crackers. Store in airtight container.

*Sundried Tomato pg. 63(top), Parmesan Cheddar pg. 62, Multi Seed pg. 60,*
*Caraway Onion pg. 63 (bottom)*

# PARMESAN CHEDDAR CRACKERS

*PARCHMENT PAPER REQUIRED*

**WET**
- ½ cup cold water
- 3 tbsp oil

**DRY**
- ⅓ cup ground almonds (blanched)
- ⅓ cup light buckwheat flour
- ¼ cup ground flax (yellow)
- 2 tbsp coconut flour (sifted)
- 2 tbsp psyllium
- ¼ cup dried parmesan cheese
- ¼ cup grated cheddar cheese
- sesame seeds for top

Preheat oven to 325F. Move oven rack to bottom third of oven.

Stir together all dry ingredients. Add water and oil and stir until it forms a ball. Let sit while preparing parchment paper.

Cut a piece of parchment paper the size of a large sized cookie sheet. Moisten work surface with a bit of water. Place parchment over (this keeps paper from sliding during rolling) then put ball of dough on top. Cut a piece of waxed paper the same size and place over top. Roll dough out going from center to outer edges, so dough is the same thickness in the centre as the edges. Dough should be about 1/8" thick. The edges will not be even, not a problem. Peel waxed paper off and using a pizza cutter or thin bladed knife cut to cracker size. Prick each cracker in several places with the tines of a fork. Sprinkle with sesame seeds then lightly roll with rolling pin to press into dough. Slide parchment paper with dough on it, onto cookie sheet.
Bake in oven for 25 minutes. Remove and break off any outside crackers that are crispy. Gently break up the rest of the crackers and place around pan, put back in the oven and bake another 5- 10 minutes or until crackers are light brown and crispy.

NOTE: You may have to take some off the pan and continue baking the rest in order for them all to get crispy. The outside crackers tend to get a little browner but they are still good.

Makes approximately 5 doz. crackers. Store in airtight container.

62

# SUNDRIED TOMATO CRACKERS

*PARCHMENT PAPER REQUIRED*

**WET**
- ½ cup cold water
- 3 tbsp oil

**DRY**
- ⅓ cup ground almonds
- ⅓ cup light buckwheat flour
- ¼ cup ground flax
- 2 tbsp coconut flour (sifted)
- 2 tbsp psyllium
- 1 tsp granulated garlic
- 2 tbsp finely chopped sundried tomatoes (not in oil)
- 1 tsp dried oregano
- coarse sea salt for top (optional)

Follow directions for Parmesan Cheddar Cracker (pg. 62) except sprinkle coarse sea salt on top if desired.

# CARAWAY ONION CRACKERS

*PARCHMENT PAPER REQUIRED*

**WET**
- ½ cup cold water
- 3 tbsp oil

**DRY**
- ⅓ cup ground almonds
- ⅓ cup light buckwheat flour
- ¼ cup ground flax
- 2 tbsp coconut flour (sifted)
- 2 tbsp psyllium
- 1½ tsp caraway seeds
- 1½ tsp granulated onion
- 1 tbsp parmesan cheese
- coarse sea salt for top (optional)
-

Follow directions for Parmesan Cheddar Crackers (pg. 62) except sprinkle coarse sea salt on top if desired.

# PIE CRUST

**WET**

- 6 tbsp boiling water
- 3 tbsp melted butter
- 1 egg yolk

**DRY**

- ¾ cup ground almond (blanched)
- ¼ cup ground flax (golden)
- 2 tbsp coconut flour (sifted)
- 1 tbsp psyllium

In medium bowl mix ground almonds, ground flax, coconut flour and psyllium. Add boiling water and melted butter and mix well with fork. Blend in the egg yolk.

Form into ball and knead gently on floured surface (use coconut flour) just until it is not sticky. Wrap dough in plastic wrap and let stand at room temperature for 30 minutes.

To roll pastry, flour work surface liberally with coconut flour. Roll, rolling pin in flour as well to keep dough from sticking to it. Roll to size of 9" pie plate. Fold in half and place in pie plate (if it comes apart in places you can stick it back together). Open pastry into pie plate. Trim edges with a knife.

Prick dough with fork to keep from shrinking (it will shrink some). Put pie shell in freezer while oven is preheating. Turn oven to 375F. Bake pie shell 15-18 minutes. Remove from oven and cool on wire rack.

Fill with your favorite cold filling.

If you want to bake a filling in it, just pour your favorite filling in and bake to recipes directions.

# Metric Conversion Chart

Liquids can be converted to liters or milliliters with the following table. Small volumes (less than about 1 fluid ounce or 2 tablespoons) of ingredients such as salt, herbs, spices, baking powder, etc. should also be converted with this table.

**Volume Conversions: Normally used for liquids only**

| Standard Quantity | Metric equivalent |
|---|---|
| 1 teaspoon | 5 mL |
| 1 tablespoon *or* 1/2 fluid ounce | 15 mL |
| 1 fluid ounce *or* 1/8 cup | 30 mL |
| 1/4 cup *or* 2 fluid ounces | 60 mL |
| 1/3 cup | 80 mL |
| 1/2 cup *or* 4 fluid ounces | 120 mL |
| 2/3 cup | 160 mL |
| 3/4 cup *or* 6 fluid ounces | 180 mL |
| 1 cup *or* 8 fluid ounces *or* half a pint | 240 mL |
| 1 1/2 cups *or* 12 fluid ounces | 350 mL |
| 2 cups *or* 1 pint *or* 16 fluid ounces | 475 mL |
| 3 cups *or* 1 1/2 pints | 700 mL |
| 4 cups *or* 2 pints *or* 1 quart | 950 mL |
| 4 quarts *or* 1 gallon | 3.8 L |

**Note:** In cases where higher precision is not justified, it may be convenient to round these conversions off as follows:

1 cup = 250 mL
1 pint = 500 mL
1 quart = 1 L
1 gallon = 4 L

www.thenograinerbaker.com

Printed at DossCopyCentre   Peterborough, Ontario Canada   www.doss.on.ca